South America

D1739327

Dylan Levsey

Consultants

Doris Namala, Ph.D.
Assistant Professor of History
Riverside City College

Brian Allman
Principal
Upshur County Schools, West Virginia

Publishing Credits

Rachelle Cracchiolo, M.S.Ed., *Publisher*
Emily R. Smith, M.A.Ed., *SVP of Content Development*
Véronique Bos, *Vice President of Creative*
Dani Neiley, *Editor*
Fabiola Sepulveda, *Series Graphic Designer*

Image Credits: p.9 Alamy/Jesse Kraft; p.10 Alamy/Udazkena; p.11 (top) Alamy/Wirestock, Inc.; p.11 (bottom) Alamy/J.Enrique Molina; p.12 (top) Alamy/North Wind Picture Archives; p.13 (top) Alamy/Izel Photography - A; p.17 (top) Getty Images/Bettmann; p.17 (bottom) Alamy/J.Enrique Molina; p.19 (bottom) Getty Images/Eric Schweikardt; p.20 Alamy/SOPA Images Limited; p.21 (top) Alamy/Reuters; p.22 (top) Alamy/Jose Bula; p.22 (bottom) Alamy/Forget Patrick; p.23 (top) Alamy/Reuters; p.32 Alamy/Everett Collection Historical; all other images from iStock and/or Shutterstock

Library of Congress Cataloging-in-Publication Data

Names: Levsey, Dylan, author.
Title: South America / Dylan Levsey.
Description: Huntington Beach, CA : Teacher Created Materials, Inc, [2023]
| Includes index. | Audience: Ages 8-18 | Summary: "South America is
home to many landscapes. Diverse cultures call this continent home.
These cultures have different histories and beliefs. Discover how South
America has changed over the years and what it is like in the present.
Learn about the Inka Empire, the Andes Mountains, and much more!"--
Provided by publisher.
Identifiers: LCCN 2022038210 (print) | LCCN 2022038211 (ebook) | ISBN
9781087695112 (paperback) | ISBN 9781087695273 (ebook)
Subjects: LCSH: South America--Juvenile literature.
Classification: LCC F2208.5 .L48 2023 (print) | LCC F2208.5 (ebook) | DDC
980--dc23/eng/20220817
LC record available at https://lccn.loc.gov/2022038210
LC ebook record available at https://lccn.loc.gov/2022038211

Shown on the cover is the Christ the Redeemer statue in Rio de Janeiro, Brazil.

5482 Argosy Avenue
Huntington Beach, CA 92649
www.tcmpub.com
ISBN 978-1-0876-9511-2
© 2023 Teacher Created Materials, Inc.

Table of Contents

Cradle of Civilization. 4

Biodiversity 6

Early History 10

Indigenous Peoples 12

South America Today 18

Civics and Government 20

Economies and Jobs 22

The Land of Firsts .26

Map It! 28

Glossary 30

Index 31

Learn More! 32

Cradle of Civilization

South America is one of the world's seven continents. It is made up of twelve countries. It also has a few territories. Before these countries and territories existed, there were civilizations. These groups of people developed their own ways of life. They invented methods of farming. They lived off the land. There are only a few regions of the world where civilizations developed. These areas are called *cradles of civilization*. South America is home to one of them. **Indigenous** peoples have thrived in this area for thousands of years.

Today, South America is a continent rich in history. Ancient ruins can be found across the land. The continent has many mountain ranges, rain forests, and deserts. Each country in South America has its own **culture** and history. Let's explore the past and the present in South America!

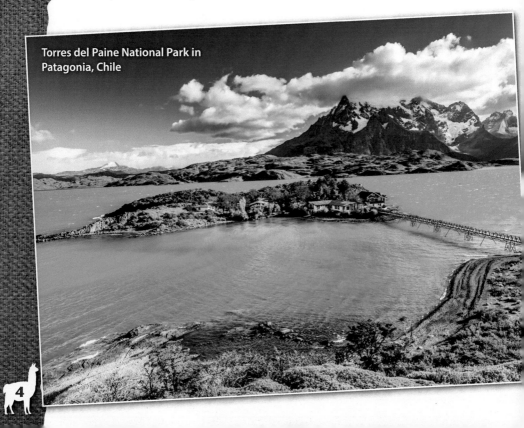

Torres del Paine National Park in Patagonia, Chile

Gulf of
Mexico

Caribbean
Sea

VENEZUELA

GUYANA

SURINAME

FRENCH GUIANA
(FRANCE)

COLOMBIA

ECUADOR

GALÁPAGOS
ISLANDS

PERU

BRAZIL

BOLIVIA

Pacific
Ocean

CHILE

PARAGUAY

AtlanticOcean

TER
ND

ARGENTINA

URUGUAY

FALKLAND
ISLANDS

SOUTH GEORGIA AND THE
SOUTH SANDWICH ISLANDS (UNITED KINGDOM)

N
W   E
S

5

Biodiversity

Land features of all sorts can be found in South America. These include vast mountain ranges, deserts, and plains. There are also flat grasslands and sandy beaches. Tropical rain forests are in the northern half of the continent. The Amazon Rain Forest is the most well-known. Temperate rain forests also exist in South America. They have cooler temperatures than tropical rain forests. They are found in southern Chile.

South America is also filled with many different **habitats**. It is home to some of the most **biodiverse** regions in the world. Many different animals live across the land. Thousands of plants live there, too.

sea lions in Uruguay

guanacos in Torres del Paine National Park

Angel Falls, Venezuela

Bodies of Water

Many bodies of water can be found in South America. South America has the tallest waterfall in the world. It is called Angel Falls. It is 3,212 feet (979 meters) tall. South America also has one of the largest rivers in the world. It is the Amazon River. It starts in Peru and goes through several countries. It empties into the Atlantic Ocean. The Amazon has many smaller rivers that branch off from it. They can be found in a total of nine countries. They make up the Amazon River Basin. This basin provides rich soil for growing food. It also provides fresh water for the entire Amazon Rain Forest.

The Amazon Rain Forest

The Amazon Rain Forest is considered to be the largest rain forest in the world. Millions of plants and animals can be found there. But this may change in the future. **Deforestation** is a problem for the Amazon. Trees are being cut down so the land can be used for other purposes.

7

Mountains and Deserts

The Andes Mountain range is the longest mountain range in the world. The mountains go from Venezuela all the way down to the southern tip of South America. There are many high peaks and rugged land in the Andes. This made the mountain range an important source of protection for the Andean people. The mountains have many resources. Metals, such as gold and silver, can be found there. Lots of different plants and crops grow along the mountain range. And many animal species live there, too. Bears, llamas, and deer are just a few of the animals that make their homes in the Andes.

High Points

Ojos del Salado

The world's tallest active volcano lies within the Andes. This is the Ojos del Salado. This volcano is a part of the Ring of Fire. This is a region of Earth where volcanoes and earthquakes often occur. Another high point can be found in the Andes. Lake Titicaca is the highest **navigable** lake in the world.

There are other mountain ranges in South America, too. One is the Chilean coastal range. It runs from north to south in Chile. It runs **parallel** to the Andes Mountains. Another range is the Serra do Mar in Brazil. Some of the land in these mountains is tropical rain forest.

South America has several deserts as well. One of the most well-known is the Atacama Desert. It is located in northern Chile. This desert is one of the driest places in the world. It can go years without getting any rain. Towns have been formed in **oases** in this desert. Argentina is also home to a large desert. The Patagonian Desert lies in the southern part of the country. The climate is dry and cold.

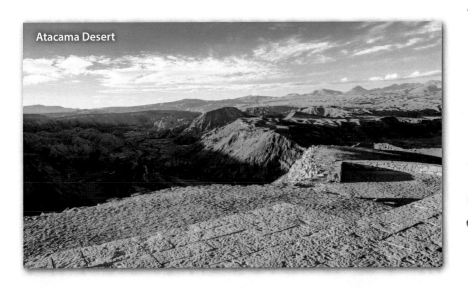
Atacama Desert

9

Early History

Today, there is debate about how people first got to South America. But there is proof of when people first started living there. There is also evidence of how Indigenous peoples lived during ancient times.

One of the first known villages in South America began between 16,000 and 12,000 BCE. The village was located in Monte Verde. Monte Verde is near the coast of southern Chile. Many **historians** believe that the people who lived there were farmers. **Archaeologists** found tools and firepits in the area. They also found simple houses. These houses were made out of wooden posts and animal hides. Inside these houses were clay-lined cooking pots. They also found many different types of plants in this region.

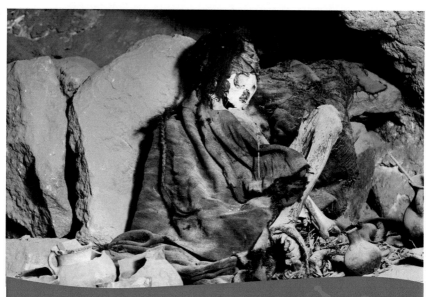

Chinchorro Mummies

In some ancient cultures, people preserved the bodies of those who died. These preserved people are called mummies. The Chinchorro mummies are the oldest known mummies to exist. They were found in what is now northern Chile. These mummies existed 2,000 years before Egyptian mummies.

ruins of the city of Caral in Peru

Caral

The ancient city of Caral is the oldest-known city to exist in the Americas. It became a city in 3200 BCE. The people who lived there became known as the Caral-Supe culture. This group was formed in the Supe valley of Peru. The Inka peoples also lived in Peru. But thousands of years passed between the Caral-Supe and the Inka civilizations. Both of these groups are known as Andean cultures. They lived in and near the Andes Mountains. The mountains affected their ways of life.

historic figurine found near Caral

Inka peoples use quipus.

Indigenous Peoples

Long ago, South America was made up of hundreds of individual **nations**. Each nation had its own language and way of life. Many of these separate nations traded and communicated with one another. Some of them used quipus to share information. The Inka also developed a system that allowed them to communicate between long distances in a single day. The Inka created tambos strategically along road systems. Tambos were outposts placed along roads. The messengers who carried quipus from one tambo to the next were called *chasquis*. They stayed at these stations until they received messages that needed to be delivered. Then, they traveled their vast road system on foot.

Quipus

Quipus were used to record information. They were made of cords. One main cord was at the top. Other cords were attached and hung down from the top cord. The type of knots used and the color of each cord held meaning. Some quipus were used for **accounting** purposes. The earliest known quipus were used in the year 2600 BCE.

quipu

The Huari

One of the most influential Andean cultures was the Huari culture. The Huari culture had state-run farming areas. These included terraces. Terraces allowed crops to be grown on hills. The Huari were the first to build huge road systems. And their cities were created with grid systems. This is how most modern cities are laid out.

Peruvian museum re-creation of Indigenous peoples

Inka terrace farming

Inka Empire

The Inka Empire is one of the most well-known empires in South America. The language of the Inka was known as Quechua. This language is still spoken in South America. The Inka Empire started out as a single city known as Cusco. This was in what is now Peru. It was formed in 1100 CE. The empire grew very fast. It became very large. It stretched a vast distance along the coast. At one point, it was the largest empire on Earth. There were over 100 ethnic groups within the empire. And it was made up of 12 million people.

The Inka peoples lived busy lives. Many of them were farmers, and they grew a variety of crops. This included corn, squash, and potatoes. They built their own homes out of stone or a type of mud called *adobe*. Religion was very important to them. They worshipped many gods, and they completed various religious rituals.

Today, many Inka ruins can be found in Peru. The Sacred Valley has several sites that can be visited. Machu Picchu is one of them. It is very high up in the Andes. People go to see the ancient buildings made of stone. Another site people can visit is a terraced water garden.

Many **descendants** of the Inka live in the Andes today. Most of them are animal herders and farmers. They live in small communities. It is thought that nearly 45 percent of Peru's population are descendants of the Inka.

Animals

The Inka raised several different kinds of animals. They raised ducks, llamas, and alpacas. They also raised dogs and guinea pigs. They used wool from llamas to make clothing.

Peruvian hairless dog

water source at
Ollantaytambo, Peru

Machu Picchu, Peru

15

People of the Amazon Rain Forest

The Amazon Rain Forest is very dense. It is difficult to explore parts of it due to all the trees and plants. So, historians didn't know if Indigenous peoples had lived there long ago. They used to think that it would have been a hard place to survive in. This is because the soil in the region made it hard to grow crops. They thought Indigenous peoples would not have been able to get enough food.

But thanks to technology, historians have found evidence of life in the rain forest. Historians are able to look at **satellite** images. These images are taken from high up in the sky. They allow historians to see a wide range of land. In some places in the forest, they found areas where the land had been changed. It had been shaped into mounds. When they went to explore these places, they found shards of pottery and other materials. Laser technology helped them see evidence of roads and walls beneath the ground. Historians are now hopeful that they will keep learning more about these ancient cultures.

The Path to Independence

Long ago, Europeans explored the world. They took over many parts of South America. Spain had many colonies across the land. So did Portugal. But people in the South American colonies did not like this. They did not want to be controlled by another government. They wanted to make their own decisions.

Simón Bolívar leads his troops in battle.

The South American colonies wanted to be independent. Túpac Amaru II helped start this movement. He led the first fight for independence. He did this in Peru during the early 1780s. But this did not free his people from Spanish control. Years later, Simón Bolívar helped Peru claim independence. He also helped many other countries on the continent.

Túpac Amaru II

Túpac Amaru II was a descendant of the Inka. He was born in Cusco, Peru. His fight for independence was important. It became the largest movement on the continent at the time. His work inspired many Indigenous peoples. They began to fight for their rights and independence.

South America Today

Every country in South America is unique. Each one has its own culture.

Languages

Hundreds of languages are spoken in South America. Spanish is the official language of nine countries. In Brazil, Portuguese is the official language. French Guiana has French as the official language. Many Indigenous languages are spoken, too. Quechua is one of them. People in some parts of the Andes and the Amazon Basin speak it. Some people in northwest Argentina also speak Quechua.

Dig In!

A popular meal in Argentina is *asado*. It is a variety of barbecued meats. The meat is typically cooked on a special grill. In Colombia, you might see *bandeja paisa*. This is a platter of many different foods. It includes red beans and rice, a couple types of meat, plantains, and a fried egg. For dessert, *alfajores* are popular in several countries. These are two cookies sandwiched together with *dulce de leche*. This is a type of caramelized milk.

bandeja paisa

alfajores

Carnival in Brazil

Celebrations

Several countries in South America celebrate holidays with large festivals. Carnival is one of them. People dress up in costumes. They parade through the streets. Several countries also celebrate Day of the Dead. This holiday is at the beginning of November. People honor their **deceased** family members and friends. They decorate graves with candles and flowers. Some people build altars in their homes to honor those who have died.

Fun and Games

Many people like to play sports in South America. Football is a popular sport in many countries there. Pelé, one of the most famous football players in the world, is from Brazil. Brazil has won the FIFA World Cup five times. Argentina and Uruguay have both won twice. Boxing is also a popular sport in South America. As a pastime, some people in Chile like to go skiing or snowboarding in the mountains.

Edson Arantes do Nascimento, also known as Pelé

Several types of dance and music are popular in South America. You'll often see people salsa dancing or samba dancing. Bossa nova is a popular type of Brazilian music. It combines jazz with samba music.

Civics and Government

One way people can be involved in their communities is by taking part in a democracy. This is a form of government where the people elect their leaders. People vote for leaders they agree with the most.

Uruguay has one of the strongest democracies in the world. People in Uruguay are required to vote. They elect their president directly. Voting is not the only way they get involved. They have freedom of speech. This means they have the right to openly talk about issues. This is true publicly and privately. Sometimes, people in this country take part in peaceful protests.

POR LA PATRIA

Presidential candidate supporters gather in Uruguay.

A Mapuche Indian woman votes in a presidential election in Chile.

Other countries in South America hold elections, too. Chile also has direct elections. People vote for and elect their president directly. Ecuador, Argentina, and Paraguay do, too. Bolivia and Colombia also have this. But Suriname does not follow this model. In Suriname, people elect leaders to represent them. These people make up the National Assembly. These elected leaders vote for a president. A president is picked when two-thirds of the assembly votes for the same person. A similar approach is used in Guyana.

Creating a Buzz

In early January 2022, protestors brought 60 hives of bees to the capital of Chile. That is roughly 10,000 bees! Protestors called on the government to raise the price of honey. And they asked to give beekeepers money to keep doing their work. There had been a drought in Chile for 13 years. The drought caused a huge decrease in the bee population. The protesting beekeepers believed the government could help.

21

Economies and Jobs

Several countries in South America have economies that are based on **agriculture**. These include Peru, Uruguay, and Guyana. Many people work as farmers there. They grow crops and sell them to make money. Corn is the most common crop grown on the continent.

Other countries have a lot of mining jobs. Miners typically look for minerals underground. This includes iron ore, silver, or copper. Peru, Suriname, and Bolivia have mining jobs. Oil is another valuable resource that can be found underground. Venezuela produces and exports a lot of oil.

In a few countries, some people make a living from fishing. Many people work as fishers along the coastal areas, especially in Chile.

oil workers in Venezuela

fishers in French Guiana

Trade Agreements

Every country in South America is a part of the World Trade Organization (WTO). This is a group of countries around the world. They help each other trade goods.

Many countries in South America are also part of the Mercosur trading bloc. A trading bloc is a group of countries that agree on trading rules. These rules are true for everyone in the bloc. A typical rule in these blocs is that every country must pay the same **tariff**.

leaders at a Mercosur meeting

Port of Salvador, Bahia, Brazil

How Are Goods Moved?

Goods can be moved to and from other countries at ports. South America has several busy ports. Brazil, Peru, and Colombia have some of the biggest ports on the continent. At each port, container ships unload containers of goods. Each container is then transported where it needs to go.

Tourism

There are many tourist destinations in South America. People from all over the world come to visit. There are thousands of museums. There are historic buildings and ancient ruins, too.

People around the world visit Rio de Janeiro, the capital of Brazil. A big celebration for Carnival is held in the city every February. People also come to visit the Brazilian beaches. Some people come to see the famous statue of Christ the Redeemer.

Patagonia is the southernmost region of South America. This area is known for its beautiful landscapes. Unique animal and plant life can be found in this region, too. There are several national parks to visit. Torres del Paine is one of them. It gets its name from three steep mountain peaks. *Torres* means "towers." *Paine* is the Indigenous name for the color blue.

The city of Cartagena, Colombia, attracts many people. The city has historic architecture, churches, and fortresses. Off the coast is a string of islands. They are part of a national park. People can snorkel and swim around the coral reefs in this area.

Cartagena, Colombia

A tour guide leads a tourist on horseback near Cusco, Peru.

Service Jobs

Tourism creates the need for certain jobs. Service jobs are jobs where people provide a service for others. In Peru, many people work as tour guides or travel planners. They help people visit the sites of Inka ruins. Jobs in hotels are also common. All the tourists need places to stay. Restaurant jobs are common as well. These jobs are important for successful tourism.

The Galápagos Islands

The Galápagos Islands are located off the coast of Ecuador. They are a major source of tourism. A famous scientist named Charles Darwin went there in 1835. He made a lot of discoveries. He was an important biologist. People often visit the islands to admire the natural beauty of the land and sea. They also enjoy watching the tortoises!

The Land of Firsts

Peruvian textile weaver

South America is home to some of the first civilizations. Indigenous peoples have lived in South America for thousands of years. These groups created art and **textiles**. They also created terraces for farming. They had their own languages. They made their own governments. They also fished and farmed. Their ideas and methods have been passed down through generations. Indigenous peoples still live and work across South America today. Their communities are spread across the continent.

Climate Change

Climate change is a big issue South America faces today. It can lead to more frequent droughts. It can also cause larger and more frequent forest fires. Governments can help by passing laws that make it easier for people to use renewable energy. They can also protect more of the rain forests, and they can end the use of **fossil fuels**.

fire in the Amazon Rain Forest

South America's present is as rich as its past. People across the continent live in both rural and urban areas. Their lifestyles, cultures, and languages are unique. Many countries in South America have democratic systems in place. Some of the countries are moving toward becoming more democratic. South American countries have large economies. Some countries have more access to farmable land. They grow crops for sale. Other countries mine or drill for minerals and oil. Each country also benefits from tourism. Ancient ruins and national parks can be found across the land. Visitors come from all over the world to see the sights!

Los Glaciares National Park, Argentina

Map It!

South America has so many places to visit. Work with a partner to create a map of the continent. On your map, include at least 10 places you would like to see or activities that you would like to do.

1. Create a map of South America that shows all 12 countries (and territories). Or, start with a blank outline map. Label each country. Label the capital of each country as well.

2. Label the Amazon Rain Forest, Andes Mountains, Atacama Desert, and Amazon River.

3. Research some popular activities or tourist destinations in South America. These can be museums, outdoor parks, landmarks, or historic sites.

4. Talk with your partner about which places you want to include. Which ones sound the most fun to you?

5. Work together to label the places on your map.

6. When you're finished, get together with another group and share why you chose the places on your map.

Lake Titicaca and the town of Copacabana, Bolivia

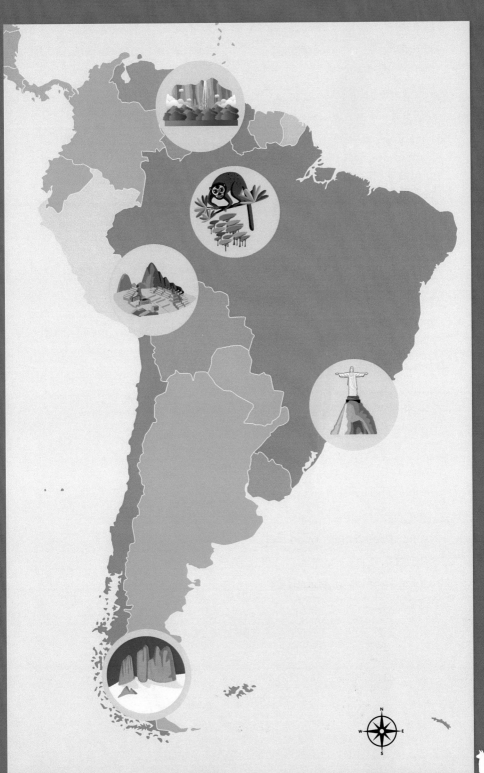

Glossary

accounting—the process of managing finances

agriculture—the science of farming

archaeologists—scientists who learn about past human life by studying objects that ancient people left behind

biodiverse—relating to the existence of many different kinds of plants and animals in an environment

culture—the beliefs, customs, and forms of art of a society, place, or time

deceased—no longer living

deforestation—the action of clearing or removing all trees from an area

descendants—people who are related to a person or group of people who lived in the past

fossil fuels—fuels formed in the earth from plant or animal remains

habitats—homes of animals or plants

historians—people who study or write about history

Indigenous—from or native to a particular area

nations—communities of people who are made up of one or more nationalities

navigable—deep and wide enough to allow passage for ships

oases—fertile or green spots in a desert

parallel—lying or moving in the same direction but always the same distance apart

satellite—an object or vehicle that orbits Earth, the moon, or other astronomical objects

tariff—a tax that is paid on a specific type of import or export

textiles—fabrics that are used to make clothing

The rainbow colors of Vinicunca in Peru are caused by different minerals.

Index

Amaru, Túpac, II, 17

Amazon Rain Forest, 6–7, 16, 26

Amazon River, 7

Andes Mountains, 8–9, 11, 14

Argentina, 5, 9, 18–19, 21, 27

Atacama Desert, 9

Bolívar, Simón, 17

Bolivia, 5, 21–22

Brazil, 5, 9, 18–19, 23–24

Caral, 11

Cartagena, 24

Chile, 4–6, 8–10, 19, 21–22

Colombia, 5, 18, 21, 23–24

Cusco, 14, 17, 25

Ecuador, 5, 21, 25

French Guiana, 5, 18, 22

Galápagos Islands, 25

Guyana, 5, 8, 21–22

Inka, 11–14, 17, 25

Lake Titicaca, 8

Machu Picchu, 14–15

Mercosur trading bloc, 23

Monte Verde, 10

National Assembly, 21

Paraguay, 5, 21

Peru, 5, 7, 11, 13–15, 17, 22–23, 25–26

Portugal, 17

Rio de Janeiro, 19, 24

Spain, 17

Suriname, 5, 8, 21–22

Torres del Paine, 4, 6, 24

Uruguay, 5–6, 19–20, 22

Venezuela, 5, 7–8, 22

Learn More!

Many famous writers are from South America. Gabriel García Márquez, Isabel Allende, Jorge Luis Borges, and Julio Cortázar are just a few of them. They all have one thing in common. They write using a genre, or style, called magical realism.

- Fold a sheet of paper into three sections. On the first section, write about magical realism. What is it, and what defines the genre?

- Choose one writer listed above, and research them and their writing. Write their name and at least five facts you find about them on the second section. You could include the country they are from, how many books they've written, and any awards they've won.

- For the third section, write a short story of your own using magical realism. Make sure to include a title and at least one illustration.

Gabriel García Márquez